LONELY EAGLES AND BUFFALO SOLDIERS

LONELY EAGLES AND BUFFALO SOLDIERS

AFRICAN-AMERICANS IN WORLD WAR II

BY TOM MCGOWEN

A First Book
Franklin Watts
New York / Chicago / London / Toronto / Sydney

For Carly

Cover art by Jane Sterrett

Photographs copyright ©: National Archives, Washington, D. C.: pp. 2, 20, 22, 24, 47, 52, 57; UPI/Bettmann: pp. 8, 10, 14, 26, 42, 49, 54; National Archives, Miles Educational Film Productions: pp. 12, 30, 36, 38; VFW Magazine, painting by R. G. Smith of the Naval Historical Center: p. 16; U. S. Army Photograph, by Salis: p. 33; National Archives, United States Holocaust Memorial Museum: p. 34; The Bettmann Archive: p. 44.

Library of Congress Cataloging-in-Publication Data

McGowen, Tom.
    Lonely eagles and buffalo soldiers : African-Americans in World
War II / by Tom McGowen.
            p. cm. —(A First book)
    Includes bibliographical references and index.
    ISBN 0-531-20189-9
    1. World War, 1939–1945—Afro-Americans—Juvenile literature. [1. World
War, 1939–1945—Participation, Afro-American. 2. Afro-American soldiers—
History. 3. United States—Armed Forces—Afro-Americans—History.] I. Title.
II. Series.
D810.N4M368 1995
940.54'03—dc20
                                                                    94-22493
                                                                    CIP
                                                                    AC

CONTENTS

LONELY EAGLES AND BUFFALO SOLDIERS

THE UNWANTED SOLDIERS

Throughout the 1930s, the world was being slowly engulfed by war. In 1931, troops of the Empire of Japan invaded northern China, the start of a steady drive to conquer the entire country. In 1935, Italy invaded the African nation of Ethiopia. In 1939, Germany invaded Poland. With that, Britain and France declared war on Germany, and World War II began.

By the start of 1940, although most of America's leaders were intent on keeping the country out of the conflict that was boiling on three continents, they knew that America had better get prepared for war. For one thing, the tiny peacetime army had to be expanded quickly. To do this, government leaders agreed that a conscription, or "draft," law had to be passed. This law made it possible for the federal government to order any healthy

U.S. man between the ages of twenty-one and thirty-five to go into the army. Before this law could be passed, however, a number of questions had to be answered. One was: Should African-American men be included in the draft?

This may seem surprising now, but in 1940 racial intolerance and segregation (separation of the races) were commonplace and widespread throughout American life. This separation was carried to extremes that would be unthinkable today. Black Americans were strictly segregated from white Americans in many ways and were restricted from doing many things whites could do. For example, there were absolutely no black baseball players, coaches, managers, or umpires in the major leagues, and no black football players or coaches in the professional football league. (There was no professional basketball league then.) Blacks formed their own leagues where they competed among themselves. Although African-Americans could be seen on the silver screen in motion pictures, they were given the roles of servants and maids; few became major movie stars. Additionally, there were no black mayors, governors, or senators, and few, if any, black police officers in most towns or cities.

Japanese troops in China, 1931. The Japanese invasion of China was one of the early events leading to World War II.

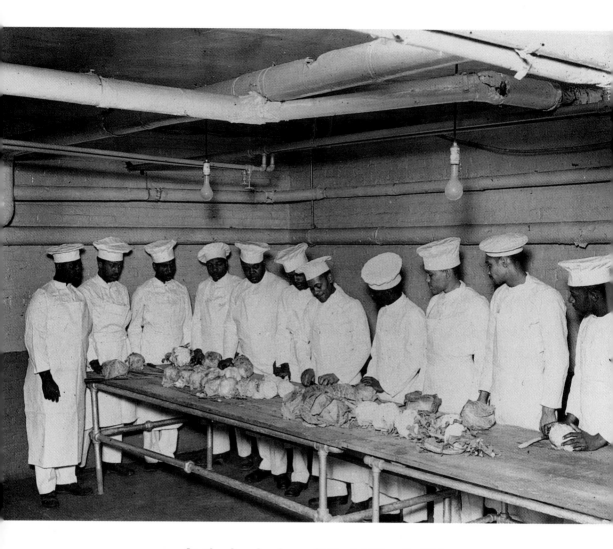

At the beginning of World War II, African-Americans in the U.S. Navy could serve only as kitchen helpers and waiters.

This segregation was also carried out in the U.S. Armed Forces. There were no African-American marines —blacks were not permitted to enlist in the U.S. Marine Corps. The navy allowed some African-Americans to enlist, but they could not be in any of the combat or seamanship ratings of the navy, such as Gunner's Mate or Boatswain's Mate. They were restricted to being Ship's Stewards or Mess Attendants, which was similar to being a waiter or busboy in civilian life. The army also allowed African-Americans to enlist, even putting them in combat units. They were strictly segregated, however, and never mixed with whites in the same unit. There were four all-black units in the army: the 9th and 10th Cavalry Regiments and the 24th and 25th Infantry Regiments.

There were a number of arguments for this segregation and restriction in the armed forces, all based simply on racism and intolerance. One argument was that white men at the time were unaccustomed to living with black men. Especially in the South, blacks and whites frequently worked together but rarely lived and associated with each other during their personal time. Military leaders, especially those within the Marine Corps and navy, used another argument for separation of the races: African-Americans would not be any good in combat. There was, of course, no evidence for this claim. In fact, the splendid and heroic records of all-black regiments in the Civil War and World War I showed that the argument was completely wrong. But the belief had become traditional, and almost no whites argued against it.

Thus, at first, many military leaders and members of Congress were against allowing African-Americans to be drafted into the army. It soon became obvious, however, that to create an army of the size needed—many millions strong—African-Americans would be absolutely essential. And so, when the draft law was passed in September 1940, it applied to both white and black men. Within the next twelve months, about four thousand African-Americans were taken into the army. But, in keeping with the army's intolerant tradition of segregation, black draftees were formed into all-black units.

Most of the newly inducted black soldiers were sent for basic training to army camps in the South. Unfortunately for these soldiers, racial intolerance at the time was more deeply rooted and vicious here than it was in the North. The majority of white southerners were bitterly opposed to the whole idea of African-Americans in the military. Black soldiers were often subjected to brutal injustices—bullied by policemen, refused service at stores and restaurants, insulted and even beaten for trying to enter certain parts of a town or city. Some were even murdered.

It was obvious to young blacks that although they were being called on to defend their country, many

African-American pilot-trainees for the U.S. Army Air Corps get their first look at a fighter plane's cockpit. Their training was strictly segregated.

The Japanese attack on the U.S. naval base at
Pearl Harbor, Hawaii, shown in this painting,
brought America into World War II.

Americans resented their help. A number of African-American soldiers wondered why they should bother to serve in the army of a country that treated them so badly. This would be a continuing conflict for black soldiers throughout the war. Many realized, however, that if the United States were conquered, the segregation and intolerance that blacks would have to endure under Nazi Germans would be far worse.

America was suddenly drawn into the war on December 7, 1941. Warplanes of the Japanese navy made a surprise attack on the U.S. naval base at Pearl Harbor, Hawaii. These planes bombed the airfields, docks, and warships lying at anchor, causing tremendous destruction and thousands of casualties. This event began America's direct involvement in World War II.

The United States went to war, but African-Americans hoping to fight for their country found that they would have a long wait. For the first two and one-half years of war almost no black units were sent into combat. Black soldiers were used mainly as "service" troops; unloading supplies, building roads, guarding military installations, and driving supply trucks. These men often came under fire; many were killed and wounded, some were awarded medals. But they were not actually in *combat*, firing weapons at an enemy that was firing back at them. It was clear that military leaders were sticking to their baseless belief that African-Americans should not be put into combat because they "wouldn't do well."

A number of U.S. leaders, both black and white (and

including Eleanor Roosevelt, the wife of President Franklin D. Roosevelt), began to demand that African-Americans be given the chance to fight for their country. Finally, when U.S. forces and their allies invaded Italy and German-occupied France, African-American units were included—and given an opportunity to show what they could do.

2 THE "LONELY EAGLES" AND THE "BUFFALO SOLDIERS"

The first African-Americans to go into combat did their fighting among the clouds. They were the airmen of the 99th Pursuit Squadron of the U.S. Army Air Corps (now, the U.S. Air Force).

Pilot training began in late 1941, and by the end of 1942, forty-three pilots were combat ready. In April 1943, they were sent to North Africa, where American and British armies were hammering the German and Italian forces.

The commander of the U.S. air force held off putting the 99th into combat for a time. The men of the 99th had nicknamed themselves "the Lonely Eagles," after a famous pilot known as "the Lone Eagle" because he always flew by himself. The men of the 99th, too, were always by themselves—strictly segregated from the other

flying units. It seemed obvious that the top air corps generals were doubtful of the African-Americans' ability to fight in aerial combat.

In May 1943, the German and Italian forces in North Africa surrendered, and the Allies (Americans and British) began to prepare to invade the Italian island of Sicily, in the Mediterranean Sea. In June, the 99th was finally put into action, protecting flights of bombers sent to attack both Sicily and the tiny island of Pantellaria, near Sicily. It was the 99th's job to fight off any enemy planes that attacked the bombers, and Captain Charles Hall, while flying over Sicily, became the first African-American pilot to shoot down an attacking enemy aircraft.

The Allies invaded Sicily on July 10, and then Italy was invaded on September 9. The "Lonely Eagles" were involved in both these operations, fighting enemy planes and strafing (machine-gunning) enemy ground troops. Gradually, the top air corps officers began to realize that the 99th could fight as well as anyone. And when the men of the 99th shot down eight German planes in one day, all lingering doubts were put to rest. An air corps general told them, "You're doing a magnificent job!" For its part in the battle for Italy, the 99th Pursuit Squadron was awarded two Distinguished Unit Citations, the highest

These men of the all African-American 99th Pursuit Squadron, U.S. Army Air Corps, fought in the skies over Sicily and Italy.

Captains Custis and Hall, of the 99th Pursuit Squadron. Captain Hall was the first African-American pilot to shoot down an enemy airplane.

award the army gives to honor the performance of an entire military unit.

The battle for Italy was a long, hard, grinding fight. Eleven months after the first troops landed on a southern beach to begin the invasion, Allied soldiers were just beginning to fight their way into the northern part of the country. It was at this point that the first African-American infantry (foot soldiers) chosen to fight in Europe began to take their part in the Italian struggle. They were the men of the 370th Regimental Combat Team of the all African-American 92nd Infantry Division. This division had the official nickname of "Buffalo Soldiers," a name given to black soldiers by American Indians more than one hundred years ago.

The 92nd Division was formed on October 15, 1942. Like all U.S. infantry divisions it consisted of three infantry regiments of about three thousand men each, three artillery battalions of sixteen cannons (and their gunners) each, and service troops—engineers, drivers, medical personnel, and so on—altogether about eighteen thousand men and forty-eight cannons. Somehow, the division managed to get hold of a young buffalo they named "Buffalo Bill" as a mascot; he was present at all parades and special functions!

After months of combat training the division was pronounced ready. On July 30, 1944, the division's 370th Infantry Regiment, 598th Field Artillery Battalion, and service troops, landed in Italy. Designated as the 370th Regimental Combat Team, they were attached to the U.S. Fifth Army, which was spread out along the Arno River in

Most African-Americans in the army were given
duty only as truck drivers or laborers. But even
that duty was often highly dangerous.

northern Italy. Beyond the river lay the German army's Gothic Line: miles of fortified artillery and machine gun emplacements, long tangles of barbed wire, and stretches of ground filled with buried explosive mines that would explode if stepped on. The Buffalo Soldiers had arrived just in time to take part in an advance against the Gothic Line, and their role was a tough one for inexperienced troops. On September 1, they crossed the river and began their assignment of pushing all German troops off the slopes of a particular mountain. By the end of the next day, they had accomplished this mission, but at a bloody loss of men.

For the next three months the Fifth Army continued to batter unsuccessfully at the Gothic Line. By the end of November, the entire 92nd Division was in Italy, and the Buffalo Soldiers had been in most of the steady fighting. They had taken so many casualties that they were well below strength. There were simply no trained replacements—African-Americans trained as combat infantrymen—to take the place of those killed. The 92nd had to accept men from an African-American regiment that had been guarding airfields, men with no combat experience or proper training.

As the days of December slid by, the 92nd, with a large number of inexperienced men in its ranks, went about its daily tasks and waited for whatever was to happen next. What happened was a sudden devastating attack aimed directly at the 92nd by some of the toughest, most experienced units of the German army. The fighting was bitter and bloody, and the 92nd was pushed

Men of a mortar crew of the all African-
American 92nd Division, in Italy, aim their fire
at a distant German machine gun nest.

back. Fortunately for the Fifth Army, the Germans did not have enough strength for a breakthrough and eventually pulled back behind the Gothic Line.

In February 1945, the Fifth Army began preparing for an all-out assault on the Gothic Line. The commanders decided, however, that the 92nd, with all its losses and with so many inexperienced, untrained men, was simply too weak to be used in such an attack. The commanders combined the 92nd's three regiments into a single regiment, the 370th. They also brought in two new regiments to replace those that had been eliminated. The new regiments were the all-white 473rd Infantry, and the all Japanese-American 442nd regiment, regarded as one of the best in the whole U.S. Army. The 92nd was no longer an all African-American division, but it was one that the Fifth Army commander, General Truscott, felt he could really depend on. As events turned out, he was completely right.

The new 92nd Division was assigned to make a "diversion"—a fake attack to trick the enemy—while the rest of the Fifth Army attacked another position. On April 5, the 92nd headed for its objective. Led by the Japanese-American regiment, the 92nd turned the diversion into a real attack and made a stunning breakthrough that shattered German forces in that part of the Gothic Line. When the other Fifth Army troops launched their attack, the German army was split apart and began to retreat. In another two weeks the war in Italy was over. The action of the 92nd Division had contributed enormously to the

Allied victory, and the Buffalo Soldiers had played a part in that action.

During the months of fighting in Italy the Buffalo Soldiers of the 92nd Division took 3,161 casualties (men killed, wounded, and missing). They were awarded seven Legion of Merit medals, sixty-five Silver Stars, and one hundred and sixty-two Bronze Stars.

3 THE BLACK PANTHERS

    A long line of tanks, one be-hind another, was clattering up a road in France. On the sides of each greenish-brown tank were large white stars, the symbol of the armed forces of the United States. From the turret of each tank emerged the head and shoulders of the tank commander, at his post, peering ahead into the approaching countryside. The faces beneath the tanker helmets worn by these men, were brown; the Black Panthers had arrived in Europe.

    The African-American fighting unit that called itself the Black Panthers was formed in early 1942 and was officially called the 761st Tank Battalion. For about two and a half years the 761st was trained in the techniques and tactics of tank fighting. Finally, on August 27, 1944, the

Tank crews of the 761st Tank Battalion—the Black Panthers—take a quick breather.

701 men of the battalion sailed out of New York harbor and landed in England thirteen days later.

England was like one gigantic military encampment. It was swarming with soldiers, and there were army camps and airfields almost everywhere. In June 1944, a gigantic invasion force (the D-Day invasion) had sailed from England and stormed onto the beaches of northern France, which was occupied by the German army. Almost every day, more troops were being sent from England to reinforce the invasion armies now fighting their way through France and steadily pushing the Germans back.

On October 7, the Black Panthers received brand-new M4 Sherman tanks, one of the best tanks of the war. The Sherman had a top speed of 26 miles (42 km) an hour, was armed with a long, powerful cannon and a machine gun, and was operated by a crew of six men. Two days after receiving their tanks the Black Panthers landed in France. They were assigned to the 26th Division of the U.S. Third Army, commanded by the controversial general known as George "Blood and Guts" Patton.

On November 6, the tank battalion reached the fighting front and joined up with its division. This was the beginning of nearly six months of combat as the Black Panthers rolled through northeastern France, always at the very front of the advance. On December 9, they were one of the units that made the attack on the Maginot (MAH-zheen-oh) Line, a long string of heavy fortifications. Churning their way through heavy mud, and under constant artillery fire, the 761st's tanks broke through the

defenses in several places. By December 14 the Black Panthers had reached the German border.

But now, something happened that sent shock and concern through the Allied armies. Taking advantage of heavy snow and fog, the German forces, whom everyone had thought were just about beaten, made a stunning counterattack, smashing into the U.S. troops advancing through Belgium. The U.S. line began to bulge backward and was in danger of breaking.

The Black Panthers were quickly ordered to Belgium. By New Year's Eve 1945, they were in the battle, which was being called the Battle of the Bulge. During the next few days, they killed nearly two hundred German soldiers, destroyed eleven machine gun nests, and took seventy German prisoners. At the town of Tillet, they encountered the German 13th SS Panzer Division, with the big Tiger tanks, so thickly armored they could hardly be damaged. But the U.S. tanks were faster and able to turn more quickly. The Black Panthers soon learned how to disable the German tanks by shooting at their treads; when the treads were damaged, the Tigers couldn't move.

The battle for Tillet went on for five days, in 4 feet (1.2 km) of snow and temperatures that were below zero. The Black Panther tanks were nearly out of gasoline and ammunition. Then, suddenly, the fog lifted, the skies grew clear, and U.S. planes came roaring overhead to drop supplies. Tillet was captured on January 9. But five of the Black Panthers had been killed and several were wounded.

In tanks like these—M4 Shermans—the Black
Panthers fought in the snow-covered Ardennes
Forest during the Battle of the Bulge.

The Germans were unable to make the breakthrough they had hoped for, and their attack fizzled out. With the danger in Belgium over, the Black Panthers were sent back to the German border, where Allied forces were preparing an assault on the German's last line of defense, the Siegfried (ZEEG-freed) Line. This consisted of fortified artillery and machine gun emplacements, fences of tangled barbed wire, tank traps (fields of concrete slabs, sticking up like shark teeth), and minefields. The Black Panthers became part of a small special force, including foot soldiers and engineers, assigned to break through part of the Siegfried Line and advance to the Rhine River in Germany.

The Panthers and other units began their assault on March 21. For the next three days they moved through scores of "pillboxes"—small, square, concrete structures with machine guns or anti-tank cannons inside them—sometimes no more than 15 feet (4.6 km) apart. On one stretch of road between two towns the tanks destroyed 24 pillboxes, killed 265 enemy soldiers, and took 1,500 prisoners, who were marched back to the rear under guard by U.S. infantrymen. Often moving through intense artillery fire, the Panthers had one tank destroyed and a number of men wounded, but finally broke through their

The Black Panthers and other American troops had to fight their way into Germany though these "pillboxes" and tank traps of the Siegfried Line.

An M.5A1 Light Tank of the Black Panther Battalion prowls through the streets of a captured German town.

part of the line, opening it up for the infantry behind them to move in and "mop up."

The tanks rolled on to the Rhine and crossed it, moving into Germany. Although Germany was obviously defeated, many units of its army continued to fight on until they were completely destroyed. The Black Panthers fought in a number of battles against these fanatical troops. Moving steadily eastward, they helped crush the last German resistance.

Because the Black Panther tank companies were "spearhead" units, at the very front of an advancing force, they were first to encounter anything, and so they were the first to encounter a Nazi concentration camp. On April 11, 1945, Black Panther tanks broke through the gates of the death camp of Buchenwald. The Allied soldiers did not know about the death camps, and the Black Panthers could scarcely believe what they found. Emerging from their tanks, these tough, battle-scarred, fighting men cried like babies as they desperately tried to help the ragged, starving, sick, and dying people who were the camp's prisoners. One of the African-American soldiers later wrote that the prisoners looked like walking dead people, so thin they were nothing but skin and bone. This horrible experience was repeated when another Black Panther tank company, farther south, liberated the Dachau concentration camp.

With the sights of the death camps burned into their memories, the Black Panthers moved on through Germany and into Austria. By early May 1945, they were farther east than any other Allied unit, and thus they were

some of the first Americans to meet with Russian army troops victoriously sweeping into Austria and Germany from the east. This linkup of Allied forces from East and West meant that the war was as good as over, and indeed, on May 7, 1945, Germany surrendered.

During their long period of combat from France to Austria, men of the 761st Black Panther Tank Battalion had earned eleven Silver Star medals and sixty-nine Bronze Stars, for courage in combat, and two hundred and eighty Purple Heart medals for wounds received in combat. Three generals had recommended the 761st Tank Battalion for the very highest award that an entire military unit can receive, the Presidential Unit Citation. But this award was not given—apparently there were still too many intolerant top army leaders who refused to agree that such an honor should be given to nonwhite soldiers. Thirty-three years later, however, in 1978, after much of the racial intolerance of the war period had faded away, the citation was awarded to the surviving members of the 761st Tank Battalion by President Jimmy Carter. Thus, the Black Panthers were finally honored fully for their courage, heroism, and fighting ability as American soldiers in World War II.

An African-American sergeant stands in the German concentration camp of Buchenwald, after its liberation by the Black Panthers.

4 ENGINEERS, CANNONEERS, AND VOLUNTEERS

In addition to the Black Panthers, a number of different kinds of African-American units fought through France and Germany in World War II. They made proud records for themselves.

In the first hour of the invasion of France, a very special African-American unit was among the first troops ashore. With German artillery shells exploding all around them, the five hundred men of the 320th Barrage Balloon Battalion waded onto the beach and quickly went to work. One by one, huge, silvery, bottle-shaped balloons rose into the air, tethered to the ground by long lines. With these whale-sized objects hanging in the air all over the beach, enemy planes could not come flying in low to machine-gun the soldiers making their way across the sand.

Another all-black unit that came onto the beach during the first hours of the invasion was the 582nd Engineer Dump Truck Company. Its main job was to carry truckloads of ammunition or bridge-building equipment, but the trucks were quickly pressed into service as troop transports. Infantrymen piled into them, and the African-American drivers sped forward into the thick of the fighting to where troops were needed most. A number of men of the 582nd were awarded Silver Stars and Bronze Stars for their courage.

Nearly half of the African-American combat units that came to France with the invading force were artillery battalions. The 333rd Field Artillery Battalion went into action some ten hours after the start of the invasion, sending shells screaming into the German troops trying to stop the advance of the American infantry. The 333rd was part of General Patton's Third Army and fought all through France and Belgium. While the Battle of the Bulge was raging, the 333rd was in the direct path of a German attack, but continued firing even though nearly surrounded and suffering severe casualties.

The 969th Field Artillery Battalion also fought through France and was in Belgium when the Battle of the Bulge began. It was part of the outnumbered heroic American

African-American soldiers of a supply unit await orders on a Normandy beach, several days after the beginning of the invasion of France.

force that fought in the historic Battle of Bastogne, against almost constant attacks by German tanks and infantry, and bombing raids that shattered the town of Bastogne. For its courageous part in this battle, the 969th was awarded a Presidential Distinguished Unit Citation.

One of the all-black artillery units in Europe was the 614th Tank Destroyer Battalion. As their name indicated, their main "job" was to knock out enemy tanks, but on December 14, 1944, part of the battalion was called on to help deal with some German infantrymen in a strongly fortified position. The third platoon of the 614th moved forward into an open field and commenced firing. They were immediately hit with a hail of rifle, machine gun, and mortar (small cannon) fire. The 614th's big guns were mounted on tanklike vehicles with open tops, so the men firing the guns were partly exposed and began to take heavy losses. Nevertheless, they kept up their fire. When a number of enemy soldiers charged the vehicles, all the men that could be spared from firing the guns picked up rifles and manned machine guns to beat off the attack. The third platoon had more than half its men killed or wounded, but its steady fire took out so many of the enemy that U.S. infantrymen were able to charge the enemy position and capture it. For the tremendous

Men of an all-black field artillery battalion prepare a 155 mm howitzer for firing against German troops during the invasion of France.

courage shown by all its men, the third platoon of the 614th Tank Destroyer Battalion was also awarded a Distinguished Unit Citation.

By May 1945, when Germany surrendered, there were 259,173 African-American soldiers in Europe. About only 25,000 of these men were actual *combat* soldiers—men who shot at the enemy with some kind of weapon—and the rest were service troops that were, supposedly, not involved in combat. But many of these men did their job under conditions that were just as dangerous as combat. Engineer units built bridges with enemy shells exploding around them; men of Signal Construction battalions repaired telephone lines under fire from snipers; supply-truck drivers had their vehicles machine-gunned by enemy airplanes; men of the Port Battalions unloaded supplies under both artillery fire *and* aerial attacks. Men of some special engineer units had the particularly nasty job of defusing mines and "booby traps"—hidden explosive devices planted by enemy forces as they retreated.

Sometimes, some of these "noncombat" service units did get into actual shooting fights with the enemy. The job of the 56th Ordnance Ammunition Company was to keep front-line combat troops supplied with ammunition. But, one day as the trucks of the 56th were moving up a road near the Belgian border, they were attacked by a force of German SS troops, which were some of the toughest, most experienced combat soldiers of the German army. With rifles and machine guns, the men of the 56th battled the attackers. When the shooting

African-Americans of an engineer unit go about the extremely dangerous job of disarming an enemy mine (explosive device).

stopped, thirty-six German soldiers were dead, three wounded, and another twelve had surrendered and were taken prisoner. For this exploit, the 56th Ordnance Company became known in its part of the army as the "the Fighting 56th!"

A number of men from noncombat units even volunteered to get into combat. By the end of December 1944, American commanders in Europe were aware that they simply didn't have enough replacements for combat soldiers that had been killed or wounded. Because of German submarines, troopships with replacements from America were having a hard time getting to France. An officer on the staff of General Eisenhower, the Allied supreme commander, became aware that there were a lot of African-American soldiers who had been trained for combat but were being used in service jobs instead. He suggested to General Eisenhower that these men be used as replacements—that they be given the opportunity to volunteer for combat. Eisenhower agreed, and on December 26 notices were sent to all African-American service units. The men were told that if they volunteered they would be sent to "units where assistance is most needed" and would have a chance to truly share in the Allied victory. Twenty-six hundred African-Americans who responded to this call were formed into thirty-seven rifle platoons and attached to combat infantry regiments that were short of men.

Many of these volunteers fought in the vicious Battle of the Bulge. Many were killed or wounded, and a number were awarded medals for bravery. Indeed, these men

Colonel Charles Lanham—later made Brigadier
General—gave hearty praise to the black
soldiers who fought under his command.

displayed the highest courage. In many cases, they gave up relatively safe duty to risk their lives in the most dangerous duty there was. Brig. Gen. Charles Lanham told a group of the volunteers who fought with his division, "I have never seen any soldiers who have performed better in combat than you."

5

SHIP BATTLES, ISLAND ASSAULTS, AND ASIAN ROADS

The record of African-American bravery and devotion to duty in World War II began on the very first day and in the very first battle of the war. When the warplanes of the Japanese navy came roaring in to attack the American naval base at Pearl Harbor, Hawaii, Mess Attendant Second Class Dorie Miller, an African-American, was on duty aboard the battleship U.S.S. *West Virginia*. The ship was shattered by bomb and aerial torpedo hits, the decks and compartments were littered with dead and injured sailors. Rushing to do whatever he could, Miller found the ship's captain, badly wounded, and moved him to safety. Then, although he had never been trained to fire any kind of weapon, Miller took over an anti-aircraft machine gun whose operator had been wounded. He began firing at the Japanese planes overhead, and

actually shot down two of them. For his courage and devotion to duty, Dorie Miller was awarded the Navy Cross, becoming the first African-American medal winner of World War II.

Regrettably, Dorie Miller was killed in action a year later when his ship, the escort carrier U.S.S. *Liscome Bay*, was torpedoed. A great many African-American sailors lost their lives in the many naval battles fought in the Pacific Ocean during the war. A great many also won medals for bravery, such as the six Steward's Mates of the aircraft carrier U.S.S. *Intrepid*, who continued firing their antiaircraft gun at a Japanese dive bomber until the very last instant, when it actually crashed in flames right into their gun shield!

For African-Americans in the army, conditions in the Pacific area were much the same as in Europe; African-American units sent there in the first two years of the war were almost all service units. But of course, just as in Europe, work done by service troops in the Pacific area was generally of major importance and was often done under dangerous and difficult conditions. Men of the African-American 811th Engineer Aviation Battalion were under constant fire from Japanese snipers while building runways for airplanes on Iwo Jima Island. The African-

A poster honoring the bravery of Mess Attendant 2C Dorie Miller, U.S. Navy

American 45th Engineer General Service Regiment and the 823rd Engineer Aviation Battalion helped construct a vital road from India to China, working through monsoons (long periods of high wind and very heavy rain), floods, and landslides.

The first African-American combat unit to get into the fighting in the Pacific area was part of the 93rd Infantry Division. In March 1944, the division's 25th Infantry Regiment, together with some of the division's artillery, engineers, and service troops, was sent to the island of Bougainville, where heavy fighting was going on. The three battalions of the 25th were attached to regiments of the veteran Americal division for the final "mopping up" of Japanese troops on the island. Later, these units and other units of the 93rd Division were spread around on a number of islands and used as "security" troops. A part of this duty often consisted of tracking down and eliminating small groups of Japanese soldiers who had refused to surrender after the islands were taken—dangerous work, because the Japanese generally fought to the last man.

In the summer of 1944, men of the African-American 24th Infantry Regiment were sent to the island of Saipan. They did so well at helping mop up the last Japanese

Soldiers of the all-black 25th Infantry Regiment slog through a swamp on the Pacific island of Bougainville, in search of Japanese troops.

troops there that the U.S. Under-Secretary for War singled them out for special praise.

When World War II ended there were approximately 1,174,000 African-American men serving in the U.S. Armed Forces. African-Americans had served on every fighting front, and many, such as the men of the 555th Parachute Infantry Company—the first African-American paratroop unit—served heroically in areas where, although there was no combat, there was considerable risk and danger. There were also some four thousand African-American women serving in the WACs (Women's Army Corps); five hundred African-American army nurses; and seventy-four African-American WAVES (Women Accepted for Voluntary Emergency Service) of the U.S. Navy. (Women—black or white—were not allowed to serve in regular units of the army or navy at that time.)

By the end of the war, many things had changed. Since 1942, the U.S. Coast Guard had been desegregated, with many types of duty opened up to African-Americans. By 1943, the U.S. Marine Corps was accepting enlistment of African-Americans, and after the invasion of Saipan, where black marines fought hard and well, the marine corps commander stated that African-Americans in the corps were "no longer on trial. They are marines, period!" The navy was beginning to mix black and white sailors together and was opening up new fields of duty for African-Americans. The army took a little longer, but by 1948 it, too, was moving to desegregate and end restrictions. Desegration of the U.S. military required not only an effort from within military ranks but

**An African-American Technical Sergeant
(now called Sergeant First Class) of the
Women's Army Corps, in 1944**

also from civilians. Black activists such as Asa Philip Randolph threatened acts of disobedience and draft evasion to force a reluctant government to accept African-Americans in the services. Eventually, all restrictions on race disappeared from the U.S. Armed Services. During World War II, African-Americans had ended all doubts about their ability to serve, fight, and command in the armed forces. Through the years following the war black leaders led the fight to ensure that those doubts would never rise again.

FOR FURTHER READING

Nonfiction

Fleming, Thomas J. *Give Me Liberty: Black Valor in the Revolutionary War*. New York: Scholastic, 1971.

Halliburton, Warren J. *The Fighting Red Tails: America's First Black Airmen*. New York: C.P.I. Publishing, Inc., 1978.

Henri, Florette. *Bitter Victory: A History of Black Soldiers in World War I*. Garden City, N.Y.: Doubleday, 1970.

Katz, William Loren. *World War II to the New Frontier*, 1940–1963. Austin, Tex.: Raintree Steck-Vaughn, 1993.

Mettger, Zak. *Till Victory Is Won: Black Soldiers in the Civil War*. New York: Lodestar Books, 1994.

Reef, Catherine. *Civil War Soldiers*. New York: Twenty-First Century Books, 1993.

Wright, David K. *A Multicultural Portrait of World War II.* New York: Marshall Cavendish, 1994.

Fiction

Clarke, John. *Black Soldier.* Garden City, N.Y.: Doubleday, 1968.

 # INDEX

ABOUT THE AUTHOR

Tom McGowen was born in 1927 and vividly remembers that the toys, books, and films of his childhood were heavily influenced by World War I. He grew up with an intense interest in military history and eventually served in the U.S. Navy in World War II. In his war books for juvenile readers, he says he attempts to help readers understand that battles and campaigns were fought for a specific purpose, or strategy, and did not simply "happen."

Mr. McGowen, who lives in Norridge, Illinois, is the author of forty books, including eleven written for Franklin Watts. His most recent Franklin Watts First Books were *World War I* and *World War II*. In 1986, his book *Radioactivity: From the Curies to the Atomic Age* (Franklin Watts) was named an NSTA-CBC Outstanding Science Trade Book For Children. Mr. McGowen also won the 1990 Children's Reading Roundtable Award for Outstanding Contribution to the Field of Juvenile Literature.

Date Due

APR 1 7 2003			
FEB 1 0 '06			
MAY 0 2 2014			